24323781R00063

Made in the USA
Columbia, SC
21 August 2018